The One Hour

Sexual

Manager.

: *A complete walk to sexual hypnosis, a perfect relationship and sexual life.*

The partner's pocket friendly Companion.

By: Clinton emscent (odoemelam)

Dedication

To the Couples, partners,and all individuals out there in love, trying to make theirs a perfect one, willing to invest in their relationships as it is a piece and gift to be highly valued, appreciated and respected.

Acknowledgment

A big thanks to Wendy Prisca Who cleared her schedule to support the book,and offered her knowledge and understanding,thank you!

A big Thanks To Stacey Aston who shared her experiences to add value to this piece,thank you!

And To you all who deemed it necessary to invest in your relationship, you do a great job!.

Contents:

CHAPTER ONE:

CHAPTER TWO:

CHAPTER THREE:

CHAPTER FOUR:

Preface:

  Love is like a string of life that is needed in every human's life.

As there are different types of love,they all have specifications, necessities and roles they play in our lives.

  We receive our first ever real share of love from our parents from the time we were born,their love is the best.

  We receive love from our friends and siblings, co-workers etc,but if you have all these,if you have all these love but don't have the "love of your life" trust me you are not complete.we all know that we have a missing rib,as this may sound as just a literal expression, there is a real meaning behind it,and guess what? You can't even live successfully without your missing rib.

Your missing rib is that person who completes your whole self,who gives you peace of life,loves you unconditionally and values you like life itself,the only one person in the world who makes you feel real and alive. all around the world many people have admitted that their partners are their reasons and cause of success in their lives, especially for men, women have been a blessing since the beginning of humankind, women have been given the power to uplift, empower and support their men! That's why it is always said "He who finds a wife found a life" or better still "He who finds a good wife finds a great blessing" your woman is a blessing, treat her like one.

However,this is no different for men,they may not tell you but you mean the whole world to them,no matter how strong a man can be,if he ever loses his true love,life becomes hard automatically.

Women, support your men,they need it ... always, he's a king,treat him like one.

"A partner is a pillar" a pillar to lean on,a pillar to trust in always.

But in all, Intimacy play's a crucial role in any relationship that must strive, you have to understand what your partner wants sexually,yes it is your responsibility to sexually satisfy your partner,BUt….. "sexually" isnt all about sex in the bedroom as many sees it,no there's more to satisfying your partner sexually,which is a key if you Must keep them by your side always and make them come for more,need you more,and yearn for your love,your intimacy, your legitimacy,your body,and your presence always, you don't need to be an athlete to be able to make your partner need your body always,No!

Thankfully,this book is a handy guide,and it is not only all about sex,but building a perfect relationship and sexual life.

Introduction:

"No relationship is perfect" that's a general rule of thumb everyone adopts only when something goes wrong in their relationships,I don't believe the creator created and provided us "love of our Life" just for us to have problems and issues with them always,do you believe that?

Many have adopted this,that they don't want to "work in" their relationship,don't you know your relationship or marriage (please note that the word "relationship" relates to both people in marriage, engaged,or Still dating,you all are in a "relationship" here.)

Just as you value your work,your business,you should also value your relationship,if you think it is just about diving in into the pool and bingo! Start swimming….no you get it all wrong and your relationship will have issues and it will malfunction always,in pools you have to take care of your pool,treat the water,drain the old one,and pump in new fresh ones, every relationship needs improvement always,you can't keep doing the old stuffs always,it only get boring! And there your relationship start's it's friction….just like your car,you don't just buy a car and expect to keep riding it, enjoying it for years as it is new and will continue being new and will be like that,come on,who thinks that ,who does that?,you see these are just the little things that we fail to look into,and when we start seeing issues,we say well no relationship is perfect.

But,why can't you take the"walk" to a perfect relationship? Your relationship is important and should be highly valued,and once you start knowing,that and working towards it,you will be on your way to achieving a "perfect" relationship,yes there will be moments of misunderstanding and everything,that's quite alright,but you have the power and ability to limit those factors,yes ,I don't believe is every relationship that can't be perfect,you work towards it,not just to follow the crowd of people and say no relationship is perfect,and leave yours to continue withering,in fact,older people has the perfect relationships, because they know how important their partner is to them,they understand what they want, sexually, emotionally, physically and otherwise,they have enough much time for each other.

And a "walk" to a perfect relationship,I don't just mean , loving them, buying gifts,bla bla(sorry!) That's important anyway,but satisfying your partner sexually is very much important,you have to take control,yes take control,and they won't look elsewhere for it.

This booklet will lead you on and show you how to keep your partner under your hypnosis always,this is a term I use,you can view it as giving them the best experience however they want it,and being in control, making your relationship a great one sexually and emotionally,if they will want you always,they won't have to look elsewhere ever!

You have to be a manager of your partner sexually, intimacy is a natural strong bond,is just like an unbreakable spell,and once you take them in the best place of the spell,never will them get out,and no it is not in the "BDSM" whatever, you don't have to imprison someone for sex,now with this book you will be doing it naturally,and on their freewill,it will work like magic,as intimacy is a spell and one you should really work on.

This book will not only go on the sexual components,but also your relationship in general, atleast your relationship is about to be a better one than before, satisfying your partner sexually is your responsibility,and it doesn't have to be some minutes sex in bed no,there are more to being sexy,and getting your partner under your intimate spell always,and this book is about that!.

And you will be achieving all these in under 1 hour ,but it is only left for you to work on it ,your relationship needs some work done! Thus the name"The One Hour Sexual Manager.

Chapter One:

The Sexual Manager,(For men):Being The Best Guy

Most at times,Guys forget or don't give attention to the basic primary things that really matters in a relationship,for many, intimacy is just sex,and you see sex sex sex won't do much good to your relationship as when you put in all those primary and basic things to use,do you know that when you value your relationship,your bond with her, you are being the best guy/man for her?, women don't like men who has no respect,I tell you this is very important,"Respect" and "value",the amount of value you place on something is the equal amount of satisfaction you will get from it.

Taking for instance,You got a new fresh road baby (I mean a Car) brand new at that,so as it is new you are giving it your whole,your everything, you take care of it and stuffs, the maximum amount of worth you place on that particular car will determine if it will satisfy you maximumly,get that? ,So when this your baby becomes older, you are probably tired of it,tired of seeing the same colour,the same type of tires, maybe getting rusty and flat,the same scratchy screens,now the engine disgust's you, when you even take up the key you are already exhausted, angry and ashamed of the car,same seats,same old everything,but once that same "old" was once a brand new baby you were proud of,you want to show it off to your family and friends, you feel high and excited when you remember a trip with your brand new baby,now this same thing applies to our love life.

You meet the beautiful lady,so young and full of life,she makes you the happiest man on earth, Make you feel you have achieved everything great in the world,you wanna show her off,you wanna enjoy,have her Every day ,you couldn't even let another year pass and boom you got married to her,the love of your life,now after some years,you start getting fed up of the old girl,you don't see her as fresh and full of life as before, things start getting boring,then you start giving excuses, you start looking elsewhere, forgetting in that your mind that she's

now a mother,she is now a woman,she
is now running a home, working on a
home,a home you two built
together,started together,you forget
that she stress herself everyday to
make it up to her family,you forget the
new times and moments,but one thing
you fail to realise will be and will
always be, just like the car that you
once enjoyed and really loved like
mad, you now see as old,but forgetting
that the car is still it's model,it's
engine,it's make,its speciality,you are
only exhausted because you have
failed to give your car , maximum
attention, maximum worth,
maintenance and changing all that has
become old , because there's always
new in the car,but Is only left for you
to see it,and implement it.

Your woman,is still the girl you met years ago,she's still with that special personality you saw in her,but you are only exhausted and tired of it all because you fail to see this,you fail to value her,you fail to see her importance, you fail to see that she can be new all day,you fail to maintain her and to be her best man!,just like the car it's specification and main purpose is to take you to anywhere you wanna go to on land,and it is still doing that,and as long as it maintains and does its purpose,you don't have to be fed up,you only have to change the parts, work on the engine,work on the car,paint it new,let it look adorable as you love it to be, maintain it and service it always,if you are gonna be the best For her, learn to Maintain and service her always! Work on your relationship! Work on it and don't give up on it,value your relationship as you would value a main income business or work,she is still the fresh blossoming angel you saw,you just have to look after her always, respect her,value her and make her new always.

It is also necessary to note that, sometimes your partner may need some private space, maybe some days or even hours that's okay,and i tell you is necessary and important in a relationship,as it will reduce the risk of "being fed up",they may want some time alone to think about somethings, projects or anything at all in their life,and you should give them the chance to.

Now when you have stayed with her for long,then that little demon shit that always tells men that "things are getting boring,time to move on or get something new" that's total rubbish!,you are the cause of any "getting boring,no fun,she doesn't appeal to me anymore,I don't find her attractive or sexy anymore,I can't do this again" hey excuse me,in the first place why did you even marry her or make her your partner?,see going into relationship isn't like working on a new project that might last for a week or a month,then after the project is done and compete,you move on to another project no, see you have to be prepared before going into a relationship as it requires a lot of efforts and commitments to strive, you don't just rush in and expect everything to be alright,who does that? , That's the reason why they will tell you that marriage isn't something you just go in,to be a man is not a day job,and that is why it is necessary to spend some time dating her and knowing her well before going into marriage, marriage is a lifetime bond,so don't go about breaking girls heart tagging it "you had to move on,used to her,things became boring" haha that's shitty man,you have to be sure first , she's really the one your life and personality needs,not just to satisfy your selfish , temporary desire and want.

People break up early in relationships simply because, initially they wanted to satisfy the urge,that temporary feeling and desire,and once they use girls,they dump them, just to move on to another chick whom they will end up breaking their hearts and will continue that way until who knows? Maybe when they are now really ready and up to the task.

Relationship is like a ladder without end ,you don't see the top but as you progress you still see many steps ahead,see,there are steps to follow in a relationship and they are meant to be taken,once at a time,no Rush,no going back,no getting fed up of climbing and taking the stey,but taking a rest when necessary….is allowed.

I am not discouraging you,I am just trying to let you know that marriage,love, relationship needs building and improvements always,in every part ,both sexually, emotionally, physically,etc, you don't have to be giving your partner the same position,the same sex style,come on, things need to be Missed up always,do it always,she won't have to look elsewhere, there's power in Sexual satisfaction,and like I said it just doesn't have to be ", sex" "penetrating" and that's it? No it will get boring with that, there are many things to do ,to make your partner need you always sexually,to yearn for your body always,to see you as a hot guy/man always you just don't have to be good in bed to achieve this! To achieve control and being a sexual manager to your partner, knowing her ins and outs ,her ups and downs,her sides, her points,her triggers……

You just don't want to take her in for sex always,there are many basic primary things that are so sexual and more romantic to her.

If you are really going to take control,be a boss and a sexual manager to make her want you more and always, initiate deep connections,kisses, cuddling, holding hands,most ladies admit to love their hair being pulled in sex Also, note that,but take it gently and easy.

Buy Them Gifts
Appreciate her

Chapter Two:

<u>Taking Control:The Guy Sexual Manager,</u>

Don't think being good in bed alone makes you able and qualified for the task.

Be honest always,she thinks is super sexy and she sees a hot guy More!, believe it or not,they don't think you're hot when you're a liar,in fact they will only pretend to be happy,to be okay and satisfied, these are little things that makes a guy to be in control,to be his woman's sexual manager, remember intimacy is very crucial,she won't be having any reason to look elsewhere,you will keep her in your intimate spell always.

Women like men who **look after themselves,** trust me , you're a very hot guy for her when you keep **good hygiene**, smell fresh,nice smart haircut.

When you lay around with a tight bursar she secretly eyes you and her stuff,she sees her property,and hers alone, you are not only making your sexual life more interesting as a sexual manager but you will be helping boost your relationship's longevity and reducing the risk of things getting "bored".

A little tattoo can get her liccle attention.….

Women love it when you respect them and thier body, you see you don't have to ride them like they are some kind of sex doll,don't be a weirdo your woman should be respected,her body should be handled with care, treated with respect and value, you don't have to test a nasty body shaming degrading position you saw on porn videos,she is not a whore! Of course she might love getting super"nasty" that's a different thing,but give her nasty easily and slowly, there's nothing more than being in the moment,take your time in there,she will beg for more ,she will always want you,she will always see your as her "best guy" and never will want to leave or look elsewhere, and then you would be on your way to becoming a successful sexual manager.

Take your time so she can feel the love and emotions, don't rush things, remember you're a manager,and you will be maximizing any opportunity you see at the moment, don't worry you will still meet the chapter that explains having them that moment in a sexual hypnosis, leaving them vulnerable and allowing you to take your time and give them a great hot moment,you will have her completely,she will submit to you so you can give her a "hot experience".

Have them close their eyes, suck on her toes, right now you are licking your favourite candy,let her know that,this is part of the hypnosis,but it will be explained fully later.
Take it slow and easy, suck, lick on her neck ,let her feel it all,at that

moment you might tell her to view herself and you maybe,on a beach together, feeling the warm weather,the cool sweeps of the ocean,the birds singing their melodies, the feeling of being in a pool of roses with her Favourite guy by her side (you) then slowly lick her up,suck and lick her neck,she will be completely lost in the moment,she will be in complete paradise with the picture Still playing in her mind,the whole scene and everything,it may be the hottest greatest experience of her Life,you will be in control,then take your time and explore her body,she wants you to!.

You will be her forever boss,she will be lost in sexual oblivion,and she will follow your commands and directions.

Sometimes,your woman wouldn't be in the mood or may not want to do your wish or fulfill your request at that particular time,but know this,if you always snowed her that you cared for her,and loved her very much when times like this comes up ,she would want to also show you that she loves you as you do to her,she may even do it against her will, because you have already prepared before hand for situations like this,isn't that great? ,You see you have proven to be the best guy for her and her sexual manager,and only you alone can make her do it for you, not because she wants to at that moment,but because she wants to show you love and keep you happy, congratulations! You have taken control of your relationship!

In Fact,she has always been in need of a chance to prove her love for you,give her the chance.

The One Hour Bedroom Manager:

Here's one of the best ways to satisfy her in bed, **Periodic kisses** . She likes to be kissed on the neck, lips, and boobs and as regards to anyplace. The additional the merrier for her. A kiss could be a powerful weapon. Use it with intensity and much of passion to ignite her sultrily. every lady incorporates a few special sensitive zones and necking them can flip her on instantly. Nibble on her body and resolve those spots,she will be wholly under your spell and you would be in control ...

Women are Endowed with rattling
bodies. there's most to explore in them.
rather than keeping it short and fast,
master the art of arousal to arouse her.
Take your time to stimulate her,rub
her, explore her body, before entering
into her. This can work like magic
once it involves sexual practice.

Understand the distinction between
aggression and abuse. don't cross the
road and hurt her sentiments.
A rough love session ought to be wild
and not flip violent. Treat your lady
sort of a delicate flower that has to be
Pampered with care and love.

No she don't like you staying there and just gazing and throping up and down mute and dumb,she also wants you to talk dirty to her, give her pictures to hold on it will make the whole thing flavoured. Don't go over it though, instead talk over with her regarding what you prefer about her, however you get turned on gazing at her naked then forth. you'll be able to even attempt dirty dance and that provides your regular sex a full Fresh start....This lends a refreshing charm to sex and it looks like new, make her feel special and needed,let her know her body is a killer.

To give pleasure to your woman in bed, the most effective trick is to stay

whispering one thing nice and sweet in her ears. As you nibble on her ear, say one thing insidious. As you kiss her lips, surprise her with some horny line. state her sexual fantasies and switch her on.
This will arouse her more and make them happy as well as help making her orgasm first! Yes she has to reach that point first,if not you are not satisfying her.

Take your woman to some other place aside the bedroom; explore alternative locations within the house just like the bathroom, kitchen, study or maybe sitting room. you can even attempt public locations to create an awe-filling experience! it'll add new reminiscences and each time passes at these places,it gives her your memories, the experience,and a wonderful smile on her face , even if she's having a bad day,see you will be succeeding in keeping her,having control,and giving her memories to always remember.

Support your efforts with sex toys, if you would like to be the king within the game then bring on sex toys. employing a vibrator together with actual sex will flip your lady on success. it'll solely heighten the pleasure for her in bed, coupled with your sensual touches and non resistable sexual adrenaline,she will be left in whole surrender.

Lick her all over and over again,suck her tities Play with it,bite her soft lips

and skins,go in between her two fruits,
savour it slowly,go down there lick it
all up,suck her

Your lady loves to be treated as a
jewel even in bed before you undress
her for a full-on sex session. Romance
along with her, let her feel special
before you begin exploring her body,to
make sure that she is totally engrossed
in bed with you. you'll be ready to
greatly satisfy her in bed.

Get naughtier in bed
Ask her what her wildest fantasies are
and check out to meet them.

Always let her orgasm first before you
do,this is your task and you are meant
to satisfy your woman because you are
in control and she's in total surrender,

don't worry her orgasm won't take
long,not after you finish all the
abracadabra,she will let out a very hot
orgasm and dripping all over you with
her juice,then go on serve yourself till
your own juice gets done.
Work on holding your erection,hold on
in there and let her have the primary
part in the lovemaking session,she
deserves it,give her the upper hand…

Chapter Three:

<u>Being Sexy…..(A walk To A Better Relationship:</u>

The qualities a woman wants in a man are:

humility ;every virtuous woman wants a man who is humble to the core, he isn't proud, he isn't boastful, because a man who is not humble cannot be able to have a full understanding of his relationship with his partner, the Ideology of the relationship will be centered on himself , every woman wants a man who will be loyal but still will gain his respect from her. A man who is proud and full of himself cannot be able to attract a good woman

Respect :We all know popular saying respect is reciprocal, but most people has used the native mentality that is a man that should be accorded more respect, that is fallacious, every woman's desires is for her man to respect her, respect her personality, for who she is no woman wants a man who disrespects her, it is as a result of this disrespect from men to their women which leads to domestic violence, how can a man who says he loves a woman beat her up like an animal does that show respect to womanhood?, he has not only disrespected her but has killed her pride as a woman.

A man who can't respect his woman is definitely not ready to have the best of a woman……..''a good wife is a blessing''.

Romantic ; obviously who doesn't love romance, every woman loves a man who is romantic ,even if he is not too romantic to her taste(that's a matter of choice) but he must have a romantic side to show, a man who is rigid in a relationship can not be able to get that sweet love from his woman because he is not reciprocating the romance.

Women are fragile, like an egg that should be cared for romantically but when you are too serious,and/or

unromantic the man tends to get the
bad side of her.
 If a man is romantic even if is not too
much, trust me if your woman loves
you,she loves you,don't doubt it ,don't
question it, he has definitely won a
part of a woman's heart

 A good listener; A woman wants a
man who listens more than talking all
the time,is just like blaabing,at the end
of the day,you might be losing your
Woman,She want's a man who is ready
to listen to her, understand her, share
in her thoughts and issues, who pays
attention to her while they talk, that act
alone makes them feel loved and
worthy, but a man who is never ready
to listen, always quick to speak,
doesn't listen to understand, or doesn't
even love listening is making a big

mistake because he will end up with a
nagging woman instead of a woman
with a heart of gold,..
Every woman wants a man who is a
good listener

Funny and cheerful ;No woman
wants a boring husband in one way or
the other he should always try and get
her entertained, crack jokes, play
around not always being too serious,
never playful, always serious minded,
it makes the relationship choked up
with boredom and over seriousness,
every woman wants a man who makes
her, cranks her up with laughter, who
creates an atmosphere for fun, a man
who has this quality is walking close to
the right woman

leadership role; a woman sometimes
has a feeling of taking the lead
role,like I said before you should
always try to give her chance to fully
express herself,not every time her man
is bossy over her, a man should try to
give his woman an opportunity to take
the lead , which will help her use that
opportunity to air her views, her
opinions about certain things the man
doesn't even know about .
a responsible woman always wants a
man to give her a chance to take the
lead, any man who can do it is actually
preparing to welcome a good wife

Compliment ;will I say
*Awwwwwn" the normal phrase of
every young lady when they are being
complimented.

Every woman loves to be
complimented even without any
reason, telling her how she looks
beautiful has already melted a hard ice.
 A man who doesn't compliment his
woman is indirectly creating a mindset
to the woman that he doesn't
appreciate her for who she is and no
reason to love her.
A man who tries to compliment his
woman has indeed melted d hard ice
and such a woman can be ready to do
anything for him at that moment
because she felt loved.
Compliment begets commitment

Love her body; Play with her body
with your hands, going about touching
her everywhere. Massage her breasts
or stimulate her down there. Make use
of your tongue to tease her and love

her. A little bit of licking will do wonders and your woman will respond beautifully to these moves. Softly bite her folds of skin and watch her groan with pleasure.

Show her how much you are in love with her body,and how her body alone makes you feel great,she will try every time to even give you more and more greater experiences when she knows you value and love her body that much.

Maintain a good hygiene at night always: Your hygiene matters alot to her and it sets the perfect scenario for good sex. Before going to bed, take a shower and pull a soft perfume. Make sure the unwanted hair is all removed or trimmed. Pay attention to your

undergarments. This will turn her on big time.
She will always want to stay close to you and embedded into your body because she feels life,she feels great with your appetising aroma and clean body.

Her Choice matters, always:
Instead of imposing on your moves, ask your woman how she would like to be loved. Place her needs and desires before yours. Give importance to what she likes and how she likes it.
This alone will help your woman shed her inhibitions on sex and help in the maximum satisfaction of the bedroom task!

Loyalty ; A loyal man is a responsible man, every woman wants a man who

is loyal, who trusts and respect her
both inside and outside, no woman is
happy with a womanizer, a cheat, a
woman wants a man who is loyal and
understanding, and trust her

Chapter Four:

Being The Best Woman:

There are prominent qualities every man desires of a woman and they include ;

Respect : Every man loves a woman who respects them irrespective of his status or position, they feel if a woman disrespects them their ego has been bruised, respect is a key factor to winning a man's heart, a woman who can give at least 99% of respect to her man is a valid to be with.

When a woman respect a man, it makes him feel his worth as a man, most men who aren't so financially stable in their homes may not actually feel so less of their financial capability because the woman he has is giving him respect despite his status and that will trigger him to work harder to reciprocate the respect.

Additionally,If a woman doesn't have the level of intelligence quotient in giving her man respect then she has automatically crashed the first strategy in having a good man and a good home.

A relationship where there is exquisite respect for a man is just the stepping stone to winning his heart

Acceptance: a wise quote says"I don't need anything to complete me, I only need someone to accept me completely ". One of the greatest gifts a man loves

is when a woman totally accepts him
for whom he is and not what he is.
 Generally acceptance is essential,it is
important for friendships,
relationships. Every man loves
acceptance. Any woman who totally
accepts a man for the kind of person he
is has gotten the best part of him.
Acceptance is a major operator in a
relationship, most women makes this
mistake which makes them to lose
their man, when they don't fully accept
who he is, most times they complain
that his not romantic, (you can change
that,in fact you can take control)he is
easy going, his job is choking their
relationship, they are not feeling his
attention because of one thing he or
does or the other , he is not too
brushed up to their taste, raising
unwanted tantrums, no man will ever

what to be with such a woman, they want a woman who will accept them for everything not minding, and these men are already to make their woman the happiest that they won't ask for another. Acceptance is just embracing the originality..

Space : This is a great bridge so many women don't know how to cross, most women think that when their man tells them he needs space they feel he doesn't want them any more, when he tells you he needs some quiet time alone,give it to him.

In every man's life , he is built up to have to create a special time for himself, that moments they use it to meditate, to think deep, to thrive to achieve more, the time to have their quiet time, to get rid of some issues, but some women think they have lost interest in them. Every man loves and wants a woman who acknowledges and respects their space. Any woman who is able to understand a man's time and space has definitely scored a big goal in his court

Affection & sexual Intercourse:of course this is the primary factor, when there is no love & intimacy in a relationship, the bond won't be firm. Affection makes the bond tighter. During sexual intercourse both can express every feeling out withholding nothing back. Every man will want to have such a woman who is affectionate towards him genuinely

Trust ;in every relationship trust is the basic foundation, without trust a lot of petty issues will arise. Every man wants a woman who will trust him, and believe in him, they don't want a relationship where she will always be feeling insecure, if a woman is able to trust her man, even if she is suspicious of whatever she will be able to put it under control and keep the trust intact,and that's what makes you a manager,ain't it?

Moving on…..

Appreciation: This is a striking key to a man's heart, a man always wants to be appreciated no matter how little, at least once in a while, when a woman is able to appreciate her man and compliments him she has touched his soft spot. Every man appreciates and loves a woman who genuinely appreciates them. Appreciation is really important because it creates more atmosphere for affection

Believe in his capabilities : A man wants a woman who will believe in him, in his capabilities , in his untapped strength, a woman who would support him and add more value to what he has already, to build up his capabilities, they don't want a woman who wouldn't take their capabilities seriously or who will turn against with their capabilities, a woman who appreciates, respect and believes in her man's capabilities has paved way for the perfect right relationship.

Understanding : This is the bonafide father in a relationship, a relationship without understanding is like pouring water on a stone, understanding is the inn thing in a relationship, a woman who doesn't understands her man is like marrying a wall because you keep hitting it till it cracks, every man wants a woman who understands his in and out can tolerate, a woman who can go into his own adventure and understand him, not a nagging woman, who never understands but rather create more issues, a woman who has an understanding spirit will definitely be a gold every man will be craving to have.

Chapter Five:

<u>Taking Control:The Female Sexual Manager</u>:

There are a few things to be in control,to always have your partner's attention for yourself and yourself alone,by right your husband or guy should be yours and yours alone,but unfortunately out there is something else,if you don't and won't be willing to satisfy your man, Truth be told he is likely to get it elsewhere,so heroine! Girdle up! And give your man the best experience always,you need to and you have to,he deserves it, however so far we have seen that sex doesn't mean you're sexy or good for your partner,sex is a key part quite alright,but everytime shouldn't be just sex sex in bed nahhh things will get boring also , there are so many sexual things to do to have your man needing you always, needing your body,in love with your whole,it doesn't just have to be when he goes in deep there…..

Let's get going and make a showing!

Visual cues like erotic dance, carrying sexy lingerie, a sure pose or maybe using a jewel butt plug can ship your guy into overdrive. The enchantment is everything, and accentuating your look via acting in a manner or adding a few visible excitement will make him wild.

Sex toys can be definitely visual and exceptionally erotic. And here, you just want to bear in mind that guys need visible stimulation too, and you really can't go wrong in case you follow this sexy rule of thumb.

Each man will normally have a fable in his innovative mind. It is probably something kinky, some sort of get dressed up or just a role he hasn't tried yet. It may additionally be associated with role play or maybe try other kinky stuff. You would possibly want to ask him what his fable is, and in case you're an inclined participant, then you might be in for something amusing or weird, relying upon your husband's personality,give it to him,have your way into him,show him you got the keys to his thing,show him

you have power, sometimes obviously
he wants you to dominate,he wants it...

adore it or not, the lusty, naughty, dirty
quickie is an element that your guy
might love.
In some cases,Some husbands like it
because they're worn-out from an
afternoon at work and just need to
have that big, hot and lusty launch
with their wife. So if you may get
prepared for him this may rock his
world if all he wishes is to feel
satisfaction from fast ejaculation
without foreplay..

 So you know,Most men dream of
ejaculating inside or on a certain part
of their spouse. And sometimes this
will be a bit messy,but your
creativeness should run wild here,

even if it's in-between your fruits or even your butt,all in there,let him have his way, if you can't do the mouth always, at least surprise him sometimes,let his kinky desires be actualised,let him feel fulfilled…. actually that's how they will feel when they nut in…..while is all dirty haha, sometimes you gotta go dirty with him,it makes your relationship a memorable one, looking back at those moments, remembering his woman's tricks and treats,no way is he leaving!

Some guys prefer to get straight to the purpose and be told, handily what their better half desires. He's attempting to induce his finish game too, therefore if you let him understand what you would like, then he'll be able to get to his half sooner. this can be the wife's chance to inform her partner wherever, once and how does one find it irresistible within the chamber or the shower, and does one prefer to be touched quick or slow? different fascinating fantasies may return to light-weight here too. simply take the lead and he would follow.

For some guys this can be sexual perversion, for others it's being touched in just the correct place. no matter what tho', you'll realize it by the method he acts or groans, or even simply raise him therefore you'll be able to take him to his sensational place. keep in mind time after time,after you did that factor he liked? He probably told you he, really, very idolised it, or he created a cheerful face or came for you. Well, this can be that factor.

Some men have quite one, and in most cases, the angle is everything, particularly once mixed with the visual stimulation of what he will see as he penetrates. He may prefer to switch it up and then he will see you in several ways too.

Some men prefer to dominate their wives and different men get pleasure from being dominated by their wives. Power within the chamber (as long as it's consensual) is a true input. suppose trying out some kinky and role plays may well be an excellent place to begin. Are you dominant or the submissive? Work it out before you begin to play.

Chapter Six:

<u>Achieving Real Sexual Hypnosis On Your Partner</u>:

If You want To achieve Sexual Hypnosis real time,be it at that moment of pleasure or even continuously,there are simple steps to follow,and you,the partner doing it must ready your mind for what you are about to do,and your partner should also know and be willing to try it out with you,after all what makes it all fun and interesting if not trying out new things, checking out fantasies and all in the bedroom or wherever be it you're enjoying your partner,is always cool to try out new stuffs with him/her and using this is pretty cool,just get them under your spell then do whatever you want with your partner try out your dirty secrets on their body give them instructions to do and they will follow your command! Whoa that's cool right?! Spicing up things usually is an added bonus and advantage of keeping your relationship alive,and guess what it doesn't only makes your Sexual life more interesting but your relationship in general, keeping your partner by your side always is definitely great and advisable ,you don't know it and won't know it, someone out there is definitely eyeing to snatch your partner,and I your responsibility to make sure that doesn't happen,this is not crazy is just reality and you know it,like it or not you're not the only one in Love with him/her and make a mistake? They are gone,this is just the truth,and when you accept it things turn greater for you two!

Okay these are simple steps to take and we will see it all one by one:

•Get Their Attention:
First things first,you won't be getting any results if you don't get their whole attention first,think about it,this is just like, you're walking down the road and suddenly you saw something very awesome and breathtaking being visualised in the sky,what do you do at that Moment? You are going to ti stand still at that particular spot and just widely open your mouth staring at the wonders you haven't seen

before,you're not going to break free
from that,you are not going to stop
staring until someone calls you or taps
you back to reality, that's it the stuff in
the sky got your attention and at that
very moment you are in there or on
there in the sky,that thing can then
control you,how? When it moves you
moves,you follow the rhythm,if it gets
to motion,you also get to motion,it has
bypassed your conscious mind which
is the critical factor you must pass
when performing this art,and it
successfully tapped into your
unconscious mind,you think you're up
there or even in it,is merely an
illusion,but there's more to it,so as
simple as this sounds and seems, this is
what you would be doing,but first get
their attention…..

Now **How To Get Their Attention?**

You can choose but this is
recommended,......

Ask him/her to look straight into your
eyes,let them relax,let everything flow
, don't force it, don't rush it, just be in
the moment.

Now just like the stuff that appeared in
the sky,give them something to
visualise,it could be a picture,an
amazing one,now you're definitely in
bed,so you also have to know their
best fantasy or deepest fantasies,so you
gotta show him/her a picture that
clearly describes or shows that sexual
fantasy in a awe-derful way,
wonderful…

Now you gotta tell them a story
relating to that picture, maybe how you
and her/him will enjoy yourselves in a
beach or pool trying out their fantasy,a
pool filled with roses, warm with
seductive scents,you know those kind
of words,you can even turn it into a
story they will deeply feel and go into,
just like when you are sex chatting
Someone, but now In a different
way,live and more sensual, sensitive
and deep….

Now you can also ask them to close
their eyes, before or after the story,but
this is recommended, telling them to
close their eyes,by closing their
eyes,they will start the process of
allowing themselves to enjoy a deep
level of trance, that's hypnosis…

•Bypassing The Conscious mind
Is simple,you just gotta let the artist in
you out,let your imagination run
wild,you are in the mood anyway,so
you can get extra naughty however
you like!

Now tell an engaging story to
him/her,one that will really get their
attention and make them thinking and
lost in their thoughts,it should be easy
because is all sexual related,and people
can easily be lost in sexual
thoughts,now harness that power and
use it for good,

**Spice the moment and story with
power words**
Your goal is to make them really lost
in that thought, letting them visualise
the scenario Asif they are there, you

have gotten their attention already,now
you have to work to really get them in
the deep trance,let them be in your
story and pictures,use much of power
words to get them there.

There are hypnotic themes to use
Bring in the art of focus and
relaxation,like I said earlier,let them be
willing to do it and really give in let
them be in the moment and do
whatever you ask,the whole process
would be more easy and
Interesting,and you don't have to try
hard to bypass the conscious mind,
because they are already willing to
give in,let them allow the flow,and
allow themselves to go in, just like
when you're meditating allow the
whole process.

Now you got all the sweet Sexual naughty words to use!
Yes! Those Sexual and hot words you know use it all on them,those naughty words use it all on them, Pepper your words with it ..
And don't forget also to use power words

Go on and stimulate the unconscious mind,
"Best things are likely to happen unconsciously

After you've done your induction to put your partner into a hypnotic trance… you're ready to give them hypnotic suggestions.

… a hypnotic suggestion is a directive given to someone to carry out before, during or after trance.

For instance, during hypnosis, the suggestion may be to focus only on your voice and allow it to take them deeper and deeper into trance.

For example,you could tell your partner,to always remember how you handle them and give them great pleasure in bed and only you and you alone can make them happy,so whenever a little devil creeps into their mind to even think of cheating,they will remember your voice,they will remember you are the only one that can satisfy and make them happy,you can save your marriage/relationship with this , hypnotic suggestions.

Don't limit yourself to only things all based on "sex" and bedroom moments,like I said being sexy Enough and getting your partner by yourside always isn't about being good in bed, being the best guy or woman isn't just only about being good in bed,so this book's purpose has been actualised once you put it into use properly,it would definitely work for you, keep trying!

So you see,you will be succeeding in taking control of your relationship and guarding it from external attack,who knows,and being the partner they have always dreamt of…
So let's still move on…
Still on the suggestions

You can also ask your partner to visualize their ideal relaxation environment as part of this phase.

Always check ahead of time to determine what their ideal relaxation environment is. Describing some kind of scene from nature works well.

As part of the pre-work of this phase, you'll also want to work with your partner beforehand to establish the goal for the session.

Working with your partner to create hypnotic suggestions is a wonderful way to set yourself up for success,so we are not limiting it only to sexual satisfaction and/or taking control in sex,other things work out,like the example i set before.

This step of the process is where you will use your vivid imagination. Stimulating your subject's imagination is as easy as describing the environment you've chosen together. So if you're asking them to view the scene of their sexual fantasies they had always wanted to try out,
You'll want to be vague about the environment, supplying only general detail that would be there and letting your them fill in the landscape for themselves
 suggestions over and over because repetition is necessary to eminate the change.

For example....

"Now close your eyes and go into hypnosis. You will feel my touch on your shoulder and that is your cue to go deeper and deeper into trance.
Allow yourself to relax more and more with each breath,And as you go deeper and deeper now, into a nice comfortable trance, you'll become more and more relaxed.
It's easy to be so relaxed and it feels good to go deeper and deeper.
Now I would like you to imagine an enjoyable day at the beach.
There may be a breeze against your skin and perhaps you can notice the colors of the water.
As you relax even more deeply, you might even find a nice comfortable stop to sit at and enjoy the view.
Smell the air as you relax even more deeply.

It feels so good to relax and let it all go. As you relax at your beautiful serene spot, you realize how positive and hopeful you feel."

An example to show you how to go about it,so depending on what you want to achieve, there's a scene for it All.

Go ahead and make your relationship a better one! Don't forget to try out new things and spice things up a little,Good luck! In being the Best For your partner.